ROCK CLIMBING

Frances Ridley

Editorial Consultant – Cliff Moon

RISING STARS

...en
...EN House, 4/5 Amber Business Village, Amber Close,
...gton, Tamworth, Staffordshire B77 4RP

Rising Stars UK Ltd.
22 Grafton Street, London W1S 4EX
www.risingstars-uk.com

Every effort has been made to trace copyright holders and obtain their permission for use of copyright material. The publisher will gladly receive information enabling them to rectify any error or omission in subsequent editions.
All facts are correct at time of going to press.

Text © Rising Stars UK Ltd.
The right of Frances Ridley to be identified as the author of this work has been asserted by her in accordance with the Copyright, Design and Patents Act, 1988.

Published 2006

Cover design: Button plc
Cover image: Helga Lade/Still Pictures
Illustrator: Bill Greenhead
Technical Advisers: Richard Sharp and Lisa Parker
Text design and typesetting: Nicholas Garner, Codesign
Educational consultants: Cliff Moon and Lorraine Petersen
Pictures: Alamy; pages 7, 14, 15, 16, 17, 18, 19, 21, 22, 23, 30, 31, 34, 35, 40, 41, 42, 43, 46: Buzz Pictures; pages 4, 6, 7, 8, 9, 10, 11, 12, 13, 15, 20, 22, 24, 25

This book should not be used as a guide to the sports shown in it. The publishers accept no responsibility for any harm which might result from taking part in these sports.

British Library Cataloguing in Publication Data.
A CIP record for this book is available from the British Library.

ISBN: 1-905056-93-1
Printed by Craft Print International Ltd, Singapore

Contents

Rock climbing

Rock climbers do lots of different things.

They climb big cliffs and small boulders.

They climb indoors and outdoors.

Rock climbers love the thrill and freedom of climbing.

Climbing kit

Climbers' chalk

Chalk bag

Climbing shoes

This climber wears climbing shoes. The shoes have sticky soles to help her feet grip the rock.

She keeps climbers' chalk in the chalk bag. The chalk helps her hands grip the rock.

You need rope and **gear** for long climbs.

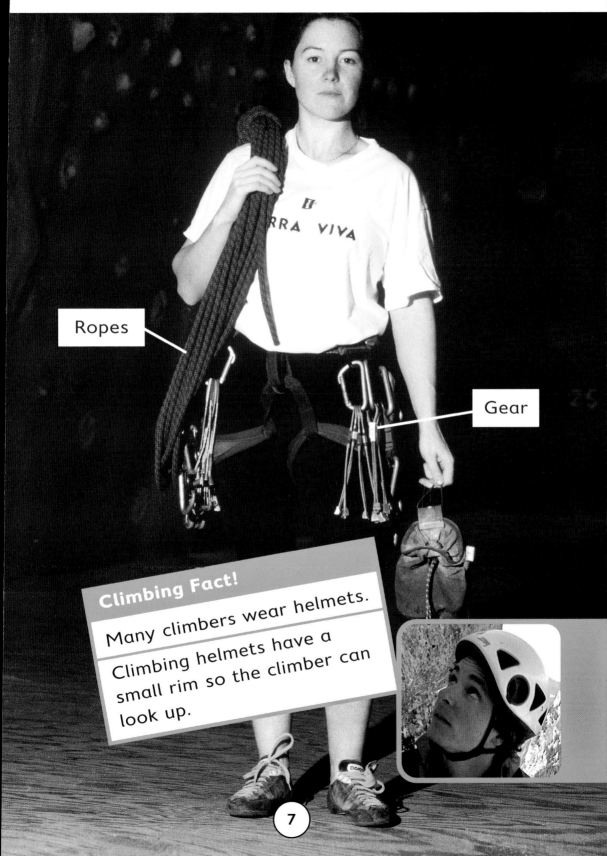

Ropes

Gear

Climbing Fact!

Many climbers wear helmets. Climbing helmets have a small rim so the climber can look up.

Get into climbing

Go on a climbing course.

- Learn how to climb.

- Borrow climbing kit.

- Find out if you like climbing.

Climbing tip!

There are indoor and outdoor courses.

Get serious

Join a climbing club.

- Buy climbing kit.

- Go to a climbing wall.

- Go on climbing trips.

- Climb as much as you can!

Climbing tip!

You can buy second-hand kit.

Indoors or outdoors?

Climbing walls are a good place to start climbing.

Climbing walls are steep but the **holds** are easy to find.

The holds are not hard to use.
You climb them in a set order.

You need good balance for outdoor climbing.

Rock faces are steep but you have to find your own **holds**.

It can be hard to find good holds.

Tips for beginners

1. Stay close to the rock face or wall.

2. Move one leg or arm at a time.

3. Push up with your legs – don't pull up with your arms.

4 Take lots of rests.

- Grip on with your hands.
- Unbend your arms.
- Lean back.

Climbing Tip!

Don't lean too far! It's hard work to pull back again.

5 Think ahead:

- Think where you want to go next.
- Place your hands and feet so that you can move on easily.

Using hands and feet

Hands

You can use your hands to grip the rock.

Climbing Tip!

Use chalk to help you grip.

You can jam your hands into narrow cracks. This hurts – but it may be the only way to go up!

This is called **jamming.**

Climbing Tip!

Tape your fingers and hands.

Feet

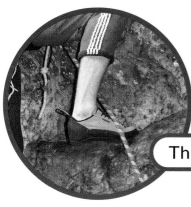

You can use the edges of your feet.

This is called **edging.**

You can use your toes.

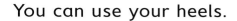

You can use the soles of your feet.

This is called **smearing.**

You can use your heels.

Bouldering

Bouldering is a good way to get into climbing.

You climb up a short way and there is a **landing mat** in case you fall.

You don't have a rope to keep you safe.

You can have a spotter. The spotter helps you to land on the mat if you fall.

Landing mat

Spotter

Bouldering doesn't cost a lot of money.

You don't need a lot of kit and it's not as risky as other kinds of climbing.

Climbing Tip!

There are bouldering competitions and most of these are held indoors.

Climbing with ropes

Protection

Ropes

Climbing gear

Climbers use these things for protection.

Protection

There are two kinds of protection.

Bolted protection

Protection

Sport climbers
use bolted protection.

Bolted protection is already in the rock.

The climber doesn't have to put it in.

Placed protection

Trad climbers use placed protection.

Most climbs don't have bolted protection.

The climbers put the protection in and take it out again.

Protection

Free climbing

Free climbers do not use **aids** to help them to climb. But they do use protection.

There are two main kinds of free climbing – trad climbing and sport climbing.

You do trad and sport climbing with a partner.

One of you is the leader and the other is the second.

Trad climbers use placed protection.

The leader puts the protection in the rock.

The second takes it out again.

Leader

Second

Sport climbers use bolted protection.

The bolts are not taken out.

Belaying

The leader and the second are tied together with rope.

They take turns to climb or to belay.

The belayer keeps the climber safe.

The leader belays from the top

Belay device

The rope is tied through your partner's belay device. A belay device is like a brake.

The belayer keeps the end of the rope below the belay device.

The belay device **locks off** if the climber falls. This stops the fall.

The second belays from the bottom

Leader

Second

Multi-pitch climbs

Rock faces are split into pitches. A pitch is as long as your rope.

There are single-pitch climbs and multi-pitch climbs.

This is how trad climbers do a multi-pitch climb.

1st pitch

1. The leader climbs the first pitch.

2. The second belays.

3. The leader stops on a ledge.

1st belay stance

(1) The leader climbs the next pitch.

(2) The second belays.

(3) The leader puts in protection as he climbs.

(4) The leader stops on a ledge.

(1) The second climbs up.

(2) The leader belays.

(3) The second takes the protection out as he climbs.

2nd pitch and belay stance

Wolf Pass (Part one)

It was a fine day and I was on a climb with Dad.

We started well.

I was leading for the first time so I put in lots of protection.

This was safe but it was also slow.

We stopped for a rest.

"How are we doing, Dad?" I asked.

"I think we're OK, Nick," said Dad.

But it was getting late.

It took a long time to get to the top. When we looked down everything was small and far away.

"It's great!" I said to Dad.

He nodded.

"Yes," he said. "But we can't sit here looking. We must get down before it gets dark."

Dad showed me the map.

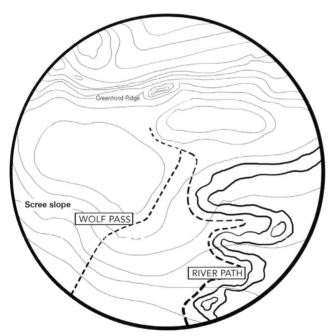

"River Path is the safest way to go down. But I think we'll risk Wolf Pass – it'll be faster."

Continued on page 32

Coming down

You have climbed to the top of the rock.

Now you have to come down!

Climbers like to come down the easy way.

Walking

Walk down an easy path.

Down-climbing

Climb down an easy route.

Warning!

The top of the rope must be fixed in well.

The rope must be as long as the drop.

Slide down a rope.

Wolf Pass (Part two)

We started to go down.

"Why is it called Wolf Pass?" I asked.

"There used to be wolves here," said Dad.
"But there aren't any now."

It was a hard path. We got to a **scree slope**.
I was going too fast and my foot slipped.

I tried to stop myself ...

... but I slid down
faster and faster.

I felt myself falling and
then my leg smashed
on the rocks.

Everything went black.

Dad was with me when I woke up.

"You've broken your leg," said Dad.

He did some first aid. Then he tried his mobile
but there was no signal.

"I have to get help," he said. "I'll have to
leave you here."

I nodded and Dad put a blanket over me.
Then he went down the dark hill. I was alone.

Continued on page 36

Safer climbing

Rock climbers can get hurt.

They can also harm the rocks they are climbing.

Follow these tips for safer climbing.

Look after yourself!

Take a first-aid kit and a map.

Take water, food and a blanket.

Pick a climb that isn't too hard for you.

Find out what the weather will be like.

First-aid kit

Look after the rocks!

Don't climb near nesting birds.

Don't pull up plants.

Don't drop litter or mark the rock.

A helicopter helps this rock climber.

Wolf Pass (Part three)

The sky got darker and darker. My leg hurt and it was very cold.

"I hope Dad gets help soon," I said to myself.

Then I heard a howl.

My heart banged in my chest.

There was a black shape in front of me. I saw red eyes. I felt hot breath.

It was a wolf. A huge wolf.

I lay as still as stone.

The wolf sniffed me. I was scared. Was it going to attack me?

But the wolf didn't attack me. It lay down beside me. Its body was warm and I stopped feeling scared and cold. My leg stopped hurting. I fell asleep.

Continued on the next page

The helicopter woke me up.

I looked round for the wolf but it had gone.

Dad ran up to me. A doctor was with him.

"There was a wolf, Dad," I said. "It looked after me."

"There are no wolves round here, son," said Dad. "You must have been dreaming."

"Maybe it was the ghost wolf," said the doctor. "It's a story round here. The ghost wolf helps people in trouble."

"There was a wolf," I said to Dad. "It lay beside me and kept me warm. It stopped my leg hurting."

"You were dreaming," said Dad. "It must have been ..."

He stopped suddenly.

There was a long, lonely howl.
It went on and on.

And then ...

... it was gone.

Big wall climbing

Some rock faces are very big.

You need more than a day to climb them.

This is called big wall climbing.

Big wall climbers use their bodies to climb.

They also use a lot of **aids**.

climber

haul bags

Big wall climbers sleep and eat on the climb.

They need camping **gear**, food and water.

They pull these things up in haul bags.

The climbers camp on a flat ledge.

Sometimes they camp on a porta-ledge. A porta-ledge is like a hammock fixed to the wall.

These climbers have spent the night in their porta-ledges.

Free solo climbing

Free soloing is the most risky kind of climbing.

Free solo climbers use only their bodies to climb. They do not use **aids**.

They don't use ropes or protection to keep them safe. The only thing they use is chalk. This helps them grip the rock.

This free solo climber has nothing to keep him safe.

He will land on the rocks if he falls.

Deep water soloing is safer. The climber will land in the sea if he falls.

Quiz

1 Name two kinds of protection.

_____

2 Why do climbing shoes help you grip the rock?

_____

3 Why do climbers use chalk?

_____

4 What is smearing?

_____

5 How long is a pitch?

_____

6 What does a spotter do?

_____

7 What is abseiling?

_____

8 What is big wall climbing?

_____

9 What is a haul bag used for?

_____

10 Why is free solo climbing so risky?

Glossary of terms

aids	Things that help you climb.
edging	Putting the edges of your feet flat against the rock.
gear	Things climbers use for protection.
holds	Places your hands and feet can grip.
jamming	Putting your hands into narrow cracks.
landing mat	A padded mat to fall on – also called a crash mat.
locks off	Stops the rope running through the belay device.
scree slope	Slope with lots of small stones on it.
smearing	Putting the sticky soles of your shoes flat against the rock.

More resources

Books

Rock & Wall Climbing – The essential guide to equipment and techniques, Garth Hattingh, New Holland (1-85974-459-1)
This book has info about climbing kit. It tells you how to get started and how to learn new skills.

Climb! Extreme Sports Series, Pete Tadeka, National Geographic Books (0-79226-744-3)
This book has info about all kinds of climbing. It covers rock climbing and ice climbing, too.

Magazines

Both these magazines have lots of news and photos.

Climber, Warners Group Publishing

Climbing, asg (Action Sports Group)

Websites

http://www.thebmc.co.uk
This is the British Mountaineering Council website. It has lots of info and help for young climbers.

http://www.planetfear.com
The Planet Fear website has a very good section on rock climbing.

Videos and DVDs

To the Limit, Image Entertainment (Cat. No. B00022PZ1K)
Originally created for IMAX cinemas, this is a US import DVD showing amazing climbs.

Rock Climbing Skills – The Basics and Beyond, Black Diamond Films Ltd (Cat. No. BD0017)
The title says it all.

Answers

1 Bolted protection and placed protection.

2 Sticky soles.

3 To get a grip on the rock.

4 Using the soles of your feet to climb.

5 As long as your rope.

6 Helps a boulderer to fall on the mat.

7 Sliding down a rope.

8 Doing a climb that takes more than a day.

9 Bringing things up to big wall climbers.

10 You don't use ropes or protection.

Index